V.M. Rabolú

HERCÓLUBUS
OR *the* RED PLANET

HERCÓLUBUS
OR *the* RED PLANET

HERCÓLUBUS OR *the* RED PLANET
Joaquín Enrique Amórtegui Valbuena
(V M Rabolú)

Title of the Colombian Original Issue:
HERCÓLUBUS O PLANETA ROJO
Joaquín Enrique Amórtegui Valbuena
(V M Rabolú)

Ediciones Humanidad, July 2004
Canada

1st Edition, July 2004

ISBN 99926-30-17-5

Printed by: Quebecor World Calgary

CONTENTS

Page

INTRODUCTION

I wrote this book with much sacrifice, lying in bed, unable to stand up or sit down. But, seeing the necessity of alerting Humanity about the forthcoming cataclysm, I made a great effort.

I dedicate this message to Humanity, as the last resort, because there is nothing else to do.

(V.M. Rabolú)

HERCOLUBUS

OR *the* RED PLANET

Humanity is spellbound by the predictions of the falsely called "scientists," who do nothing but fill Humanity with lies. Scientists distort the truth.

Let us speak of Hercólubus or the Red Planet, which makes its unrelenting orbit toward the Earth. According to some accounts, scientists have calculated its weight and measured its diameter. They say it weights so many tons, as if it was some child's toy. It is not so. Hercólubus or the Red Planet is 5 or 6 times larger than Jupiter. It is an enormous planet, and nothing can stop or divert it.

Hercólubus is already here! It is the beginning of the end for the Earth, and the Earthlings think of Hercólubus as a toy.

Humanities from other planets in our solar system already know about this catastrophe. They are very keen to help us in order to avoid the cataclysm. But, no one can stop it; because this is the punishment we deserve to end so much evilness.

Each planet, each world, has its Humanity. I am letting it be known that Hercólubus is a creation, like our own world; it has a Humanity as perverse as ours inhabiting it. Thus, the scientist lords should not believe, that they may attack Hercólubus and disintegrate it, because Hercólubus' humanity, too, has weapons. They would retaliate and wipe us out in the blink of an eye. If attacked, they will defend themselves and our end will be far quicker.

It comes to pass that in the to-and-fro of life, everything returns to its beginning or to its end. In Atlantis, the same thing happened, although to a lesser degree. In this cyclical return, our planet cannot even bear Hercólubus to pass close by; to shatter into pieces. This is unknown to the scientific lords, because they believe themselves to be very powerful with their weapons, capable of destroying such a giant. They are very wrong.

The disintegration of the famous Tower of Babel the scientists have built will happen in a short time. They have already finished it. The negative consequences now come for all Humanity.

The scientists can deny this with their theories, as they are doing and have done, distorting the truth out of nothing more than pride, vanity, and the desire for power. They will laugh like braying donkeys, because they are incapable of measuring the consequences of their actions; they plagued planet Earth with atomic bombs to take control of it and they failed to take into account that God and his Justice exist. God will level everything! You cannot speak to beasts about God because they bray. They deny God with their deeds. Scientists believe themselves to be gods. This is not so.

Those so-called powerful nations will be brought to ruins, both economically and morally, because money will soon disappear. Hunger and misery will finish them off. Those nations will not withstand an upheaval and they will be left petrified with fright and terror. Then, they will truly realize that the Divine Justice exists to punish perversity.

The whole world is currently caught up in seeking money at all costs. Exactly the same happened in Atlantis. The god of that epoch was money, which is portrayed by the religions as a golden calf.

Likewise in this epoch, money is god. Humanity is totally mistaken.

The rich, who howl with so much power now, will be the most unfortunate because with no one to sell to or buy from, they will be able to do nothing with their huge sums of money. They will get down on their knees crying, begging for a dish of food, and they will howl like dogs.

When Hercólubus gets closer to Earth, when it sets a par with the Sun, lethal epidemics will begin to spread all over our planet. The doctors and official science will not know what kind of illnesses they are or how to cure them. They will be helpless before such epidemics. Because of the overwhelming hunger and the unbearable heat, life on our planet will begin to disappear and then Humanity shall have to eat their fellow beings' cadavers.

The moment of tragedy, of darkness, will come: tremors, earthquakes and tidal waves. Human beings will become mentally unbalanced because they will not be able to eat or sleep. In the face of danger, the totally insane masses will throw themselves over the precipice.

This human race will disappear. There will be no life left on the planet. The land will sink into the ocean, because this Humanity has reached the greatest degree of perversity. They even want to pass on their evil to other planets; something that they will not be allowed to do.

The scientists and the whole world are full of panic, even though the destruction has not yet begun, but the fear of God does not exist in any Earthling. Scientists believe that they are the lords and masters of life, that they are powerful. Now they will see that there is indeed Divine Justice, which judges us according to our deeds.

What I affirm in this book is a very short-term prophecy, because I have evidence about the end of the planet. I know it. I am not attempting to fright, but to forewarn, because I feel sorrow for this poor Humanity. Since these events are coming soon, there is no time to waste in illusory things.

THE ATOMIC TESTS
AND THE OCEAN

We are in a blind alley.

We have already spoken of Hercólubus, rather superficially, so as to not frighten or alarm people. Let us consider another destructive, deadly danger caused by the atomic tests in the ocean, which no one can hinder.

There are large, very profound cracks along the seabed already making contact with the fire inside the Earth. These cracks are due entirely to the atomic tests that scientists and their countries -believing themselves powerful- are carrying out without measuring the consequences of the barbaric acts they have committed and are committing against our planet and Humanity.

The inner fire of the Earth has already begun to make contact with the seawater. Cyclones have begun to appear. The gringo lords call these a phenomenon of El Niño. It is not El Niño, but the contact of the inner fire of the Earth with the seawater, which is spreading through the ocean. As more cracks develop, there will be tidal waves, earthquakes: horrifying things in the ocean and on the land. The axis of the Earth is already out of its position because of the tests, and with tremors, earthquakes and tidal waves, it will finally slip away and the sinking will come. No coastal city shall escape being swept away into the ocean.

Do you disbelieve, my dear reader that the grounds will sink suddenly. This is a long, slow, and distressing painful process humanity must undergo. The lands will sink into the ocean, piece by piece, until it reaches its end.

The scientific lords cannot calculate the outcome of the atrocities they have committed against Creation, because they, too, will be victims of their own inventiveness. Monsters, savage beasts, already exist in the ocean's bottom, gestated and nourished with this atomic energy. They have become atomic beasts. The heating of the seawaters will make them rise and seek refuge; they will ascend on the coastal cities. They will raze everything: houses, buildings, ships and people. Man-made bullets will be of no use, except to enrage them even more. What I am saying here will happen soon.

And this is not all. From the contact of the seawaters with the inner fire, an awesome vapor will emerge from the boiling waters. Then planes shall not fly, nor ships sail and these vapors will cloud the sun. Total darkness will come and life on our planet will end.

Dear readers, I do not advise you to flee, because there is no safe place to go.

The scientific lords ignore the consequences they provoked with their atomic explosions and experiments in the ocean. Therefore, no matter how scientific they may be, they are ignorant, savage beasts who invent devices, which destroy humanity and themselves.

The atomic energy has contaminated the whole ocean and its inhabitants. Thus, when we nourish ourselves with fish or other marine animals, we contaminate ourselves as well. It is advisable not to consume them.

The ocean, being a living body, inhales and exhales. When exhaling, it pollutes the oxygen we breathe and all vegetation. This widespread contamination will cause the mutation of human organisms; monstrous children will be born that will shock the entire world.

Everything first crystallizes in the Superior Dimensions and later in the physical realm. If one looks in other superior dimensions, our planet has already disappeared from there. What we see is a yellow-colored quagmire, like a pot of boiling clay and water, devoid of any life. No life of any species is seen there, neither plants, nor animals, nor humans. It only remains for this cataclysm to occur in the Third Dimension or physical world for all to disappear.

The scientists and intellectuals will laugh out loud like donkeys braying about what I say, but when the moment of tragedy arrives they will be the most cowardly ones. They will cry, not knowing what to do or where to go.

Then, what do we expect from humanity? We await its end. The gentlemen who falsely call themselves scientists are indeed scientists, but destructive: they are not constructive because they use science for destroying all life.

I ask the scientist lords, who are the ones that bray so hard, what formula do you find to avoid the problems that are threatening to destroy humanity and our planet. No formula exists and so we await the cataclysm. Or if you have an effective formula, can you let us know about it?

THE EXTRATERRESTRIALS

I have seen magazines and movies put out by the gringo gentlemen, wanting people to believe the non-existence of Extraterrestrials, but they are wrong. They cannot block my sight. They cannot fool me and there is even lesser chance of them making me believe their silly theories and mean imaginations, as they are doing with humanity.

Just as they are doing with Hercólubus as it rapidly approaches Earth, putting it down, even daring to give the weight and the measurement of it. They are doing the same with the Extraterrestrials. They want people to believe that Extraterrestrials are like gorillas, animals. It is a great lie! It is one hundred percent false, because the inhabitants of the others planets of our solar system and galaxy are Super-Beings and wise.

I have dealt with extraterrestrials many times. I have been to Venus and Mars conscionably moving in my Astral Body and I can faithfully testify to what marvels their inhabitants are. I lack the words to describe their Wisdom, culture, and their angelic way of life.

Life on Planet Venus

The soil on Venus is not compact or heavy like that on Earth, but is rather a light, soft soil. The stones differ from ours as well; they lack the density of our minerals. On Venus, one can lift a stone that would weigh tons on Earth, because the rocks are light and made of a soft material.

The trees are not giants, and the vegetation has no thorns. No bindweeds block the way in the mountains. One can go to those mountains without needing to carry a machete or knife, because there is nothing to cut. There are no dangers anywhere.

With regards to the ocean, it is completely blue, like a very quiet lagoon that is utterly still. The ocean has no tide; without waves, one can see into its depths without needing any artificial device. The fish are extremely tame and unafraid of people. There are sectors in the ocean where the inhabitants nourish the fish with many vitamins. When they need to consume one, the Venusians see which one is the largest or which one they wish to use, and put it into a net carefully, without frightening other fishes. Then they take them out and gut them.

The fish are transported to a revolving tank of very clean waters by means of pulleys and they go through a unique cleaning process. This is done without touching them with the hands. The fish then are pulverized and natural vitamins are added. Fish are one of the foods Venusians eat. Venusians do not eat another kind of meat.

Fruit trees are grown on the flat roofs of the houses, in plant pots, with soil that has been well fertilized, so that they bear fruit. Venusians wait for the fruit to be well seasoned, ripened before plucking them. They pick them with a device without touching the fruit with their hands. Then the fruits go through pipelines to some very clean revolving water tanks, where they undergo special cleaning. After being washed, they go through another tube to some machines, where they are pulverized. From there they pass them on to another container, where more natural vitamins, but no chemicals, are added. Afterward, the product is packed hermetically for later consumption.

The Venusians are astonishingly intelligent and have perfect bodies: wide or broad foreheads, blue eyes, straight nose, and blonde hair. They all measure about 1.30 to 1.40 meters in height. They are the same height. All of them have angelic figures; no deformity or obesity is known among them. There is perfection in the men and women, because the planet and its humanity are ascending, superior. You do not see monstrous people there, as you do here.

They wear wide belts covered with red, blue and yellow buttons, which blink on and off like a beacon. When they find themselves in danger, Venusians press a master button resembling our own belt buckles. Just by pressing it, a circle of fire is formed around them, capable of disintegrating any bullet or anything else that comes against it.

While visiting Venus, I came across a hand-held, pocket-sized weapon, like a pack of large cigarettes; just by pressing a button on this device, it can blow up a hill, no matter how large it might be, and make it disappear. What would an Earthling do with a weapon like that?

When one thinks of asking them a question, they

answer the question without you needing to utter a word, in whatever language it may be, because they speak all languages perfectly. They have the Gift of tongues.

When one is talking with a Venusian, the others carry on with their work, and run their errands without stopping. They are not like us, we crowd around to look and criticize a person who has a physical defect. I have seen myself on Venus, compared my body with theirs, and was ashamed, because I looked like a gorilla compared to them. Venusians, however, pay no attention to this; everyone passes unnoticed without any expressions of surprise. It is a never seen culture.

Venusians have what we would describe as restaurants, where they go and they sit at a table. Since all of the inhabitants read minds, there is no need to ask for the food that they want. The dish arrives without you having to utter a word. They do not use the courtesies and the like we use on Earth. On Venus, you eat, you get up from your table, and you do not have to ask how much is owed, or give thanks. All of them indicate their appreciation with a movement of the head.

The clothing stores are exactly the same. When Venusians want to change their clothes, they go to a clothing store and are immediately given clean clothes and shoes. They press a button on a wall and a darkened room is formed where they change. If they wish to bathe, they press another button in the room and a jet of water comes out. The removed clothing is handed in immediately, in order for them to go through a special cleaning process. All Venusians wear the same clothing and footwear.

No one owns a house on Venus. When a Venusian couple wants to sleep or rest, they press a button on a house or building, and a darkened room is formed. They press another button and out comes a bed, without any need to say 'this is mine'. They ask no one for permission.

The streets of Venus are not like ours. Avenues move like an electrical escalator. There are no accidents of any kind because everything is in order. The vehicles are very pretty, very decorated platforms. The platforms depart and arrive at their destination. Then people do not get down from the platform up high, but the whole platform descends with the people, and another platform then comes up that is already loaded with other people, ready to

continue their trip. Those streets are moved by solar energy, as is all of the machinery. No one uses
oil or gasoline or anything that pollutes over there.
Thus there is no pollution on Venus.

In order to build houses or buildings, Venusians do
not climb up high many meters above the ground
to work. They all work from the ground up. The
roof of the building is the first thing that they make,
then they use rollers to raise this structure and they
continue constructing the next floor. When it is finished, they raise it again with the rollers, and so on,
depending on the number of floors that they want
to make, without any danger of accidents.

Venusians of both sexes, work two hours a day,
each in their profession. On Venus, there is no
money and no one is the owner of anything; everyone has the right to everything. They work for everyone else. There is no Mr. So and So or Lord
Such and Such because there is equality. The law
is to work two hours a day, to avoid hunger and
poverty.

With the inner powers and Spiritual Faculties that
they possess, they put nature to work for them:
they make it rain when they want; they make the

Sun come out when they want, and they dim it when they want. Venusians, unlike us, are not under nature's command.

Venusians are free to go where they please, they do not need to ask: 'Can I borrow a spaceship to go to another planet?' No! Every Venusian can take a spaceship from the station where they are to go wherever they want, be another planet or another galaxy, without asking anyone. They must return the spaceship to where they found it upon their return, so someone else can use it. There is total freedom. There are no frontiers or paperwork of any kind.

Let it be known that on Venus there are no families as there are on our planet. There are only couples. Venusians do not have churches or priests to marry them. Venusian couples unite for life with their twin soul or their better half as is said here, which is the complement of each human being. There are no religions of any kind. The only religion they practice is the mutual respect for life and others.

Fornication does not exist as it does on Earth, since Earthlings are worst than beasts in that sense. Venusians practice what Gnosis teaches: Scientific

Chastity or Transmutation of the Sexual Energies. That is how they prolong their lives as long as they want to, because the Sexual Energy is one's very life. Yet on our planet, we see the aging effects of fornication on people at an early age.

Upon shaking hands with them you feel an electric shock that shakes you, as if you were receiving energy, because they are chaste. Chastity gives them that energy. They are not fornicators like people here. Scientific Chastity gives them that energy.

The couple unites sexually to create a child without the act of fornication. The release of a spermatozoon is sufficient to provide a Soul, if it wants to come to prepare itself, with a physical body. There is no sexual degeneration as there is on Earth, where the priest lords are marrying homosexuals. Homosexuality does not exist among the Venusians. They are true men and women. Sexual atrocities like these exist only in our planet. Humanities of other planets know how to sexually reproduce without committing the act of fornication.

When a child is born, he is transferred to a clinic with all the necessary care, where he receives special nourishment until he reaches the age to study. When he is old enough to begin his formation, he goes to a college, which is an immense workshop where he will learn what is necessary in a practical way. The Masters of that college teach him how to handle the machinery and allow him to develop the ideas he has in order to study which vocation his soul brought with it.

When the child has an idea to make something, the professors or masters help him to develop the concept until he succeeds in making the device that he wants. They go on in that way successively with all of Humanity in Venus. Therefore, on Venus there are no ignorants; all are prepared for material and spiritual ascent.

Life on Planet Mars

Life on Mars is exactly the same as life on Venus. There is freedom in everything. The Martians can move themselves to any place of the planet without any need for paperwork or passports. Wherever they go there is a place to sleep, food to eat, and clothing to change into. They find anything that they need anywhere on Mars, because there are no frontiers, but complete freedom, as it is on other planets of our Solar System.

The Martian has a heavier body than the Venusian, apparently sturdier because they belong to the Ray of Strength.

On Mars everyone wears a soldier's uniform: a shield, a helmet and a suit of armor. All of those vestments of war are made from a material similar to bronze. They have distinguished themselves because they are one hundred percent warriors, but not warriors, as we would understand here. There are no wars between themselves or with other planets. Their war is to combat against the forces of evil.

Let it be known that on those planets nobody works using brute force as we do on our planet. Nobody sweats, and they do not get tired because the machines, which are all powered by solar energy, do the work. What the people do is guide or drive these machines. They go relieving each other from work. Everything moves by means of the Wisdom they have.

The extraterrestrials are so powerful that they are born, grow, and die, at will. When they get tired of having a physical body for many years and they want to change it for a new one, they die. When the body dies, they place the body inside a cavity within the walls, exactly the same size as the body. Afterward, they close a little door and press a button, and in a matter of minutes the body is reduced to ashes. If the body is not totally dead, then the button does not function and the body is removed to finish the dying process. There are no cemeteries; the ashes are thrown to a tree or are buried. Nobody cries because a person died. Death for them is like a change of cloth, nothing more.

On those worlds there is no involution in the plants, animals, humanity or planets. Everything is ascending. Here, on the other hand, we descend with the whole planet. The facts are demonstrating it. Those planets do not have plagues such as flies, gnats or mosquitoes, which damage health, nor is there the threat of reptiles and other dangerous beasts.

The law on Mars and on the other planets is of mutual respect: for themselves, for others, for life and for everything. They respect each person's free will. They are not like the Earthlings, who want to take over the world by dint of bullets and threats. The gringo lords are very mistaken with their movies and magazines about extraterrestrial life.

I have described the life in other planets briefly, to make the Americans see that they know nothing of what they portray, because they deny that there is life elsewhere.

I do not use telescopes or artificial means to obtain my knowledge of the Universe. I know how to manage my Internal Bodies with full and conscionable will. Gnosis gave me the keys. I put into practice what Gnosis taught me and the result is this: to know, because he who knows is the one who has knowledge. He who does not have knowledge is the one who speaks about what he does not know. Practical Gnosis cannot be compared with anything. It surpasses all the barriers and the walls that stand on the way to our Liberation.

The Interplanetary Spaceships

I move now to the interplanetary spaceships, which scientists either ignore or question, making humanity doubt the existence of such ships.

All the Interplanetary spaceships are moved by solar energy. They are made of a bulletproof material that does not exist on Earth. Nothing can penetrate them. Spaceships are made of one piece. They do not have welds, attachments or rivets. They are conduced by the means of buttons.

The spaceships have two horizontal tubes made of another material that does not exist on our planet. The material is light, very similar to aluminum, but brighter and stronger. These tubes go through the spaceship from front to back. The solar energy enters at the front of the ship. The burnt energy is expelled through the back. These are the tails of fire that the Interplanetary Spaceships leave wherever they go.

The spaceships are not all round. A cigar-shaped, long model exists, capable of transporting hundreds of people. So then, not all spaceships are the same model or the same size. These are the vehicles of transportation in other planets. The crews on these spaceships communicate with each other telepathically, without any need for telephones or televisions and the like. They have all their Spiritual Faculties awakened.

The poor ignorant Earthlings, who bray heartily, like the gringo lords, scientists and other powerful countries, are ignoring the marvels that exist in other planets.

The extraterrestrials' interplanetary spaceships are ready now to take off and rescue all those people who are working with the formula that is given in this book. Extraterrestrials know everything. There is no need to call them because they already know us inside out. When the moment arrives, the rescue will be done in their Spaceships. Few persons will achieve it to be rescued. Those that will can be counted on the fingers of the hands, because nobody wants to work. People take everything to the mind and from the mind come theories, it is the same Ego, which brings them out, and what we need are facts: we need to begin the spiritual work once and for all.

My goal in writing this narrative is to let the whole world know the truth at long last. We are not the only inhabitants of our solar system and our galaxy. We are the most inferior ones! The countries that believe themselves, to be great powers, and think they know all, demonstrate just the opposite by their deeds. The quality of our humanity is revealed by the atrocities that they are committing against themselves and against others. Do not tell me the tales they fabricate, because I do know the truth!

That is why I have written this book, so that humanity can see that the gringo lords and the scientific lords have humanity wrapped up in vile lies and threats. Truth is all that I am saying, and it is what I defend at all times. If I have to die to uphold the truth, then I will die.

THE DEATH

This chapter is esoterically entitled 'The Death,' because he who begins to disintegrate his Psychological Defects begins to leave the circle in which all of humanity is stuck.

When a person is working in the disintegration of his Psychological Defects, and is invited to do some mischief, people comment, "he is useless, he is dead." This person behaves differently, because he does not follow the ways of the rest of humanity.

Every human being bears within a Divine Spark that is called Soul, Buddhata or Essence. Well, it has different names; but in reality it is a Divine Spark, which impels us and gives us the strength to embark in the spiritual work, like that which I will teach you. That Essence or Soul is trapped within all of our evilness, defects or psychological selves, which esoterically is called Ego. Those selves are the ones that do not allow the Essence to manifest itself freely, because they are the ones that cry out noisily and take control of the person.

Now, with the work of the disintegration of the defects or selves the Essence goes growing, it becomes stronger; it goes manifesting itself with more clarity, with more strength. It goes converting into one's Soul. As an example, a tree stands on its main roots. The main roots do not nourish it, but only keep it standing against the winds and its own weight so that it does not fall, or topple over. The tiny feeder roots are the ones that spread out over the surface of the soil, and go absorbing the nutrients to nourish it.

The Ego does the same within us or within human-ity. The thick roots sustaining the tree symbolize the cardinal defects, like lust, revenge, anger, pride and others. The small feeder roots represent the details, those diminutive manifestations that are part and feeders of cardinal defects. We do not believe those details to be defects at all, and yet they feed the Ego. The Ego is nourished by all those diminu-tive details, which we have in large quantities.

We must begin to psychologically observe our-selves to see the thousands and thousands of nega-tive details we have, which are the ones that feed the Ego. This is what we must do to save ourselves from the disaster. One must begin to remove the tiny feeder roots that nourish that tree. Negative details are bad thoughts, hatred, the envy that one feels against other people, taking or stealing coins and insignificant things, telling lies, saying words full of pride, ambition and greed. One must begin in earnest to disintegrate all those details deep within us that are so negative.

There is another Divine Spark within us that is called the Divine Mother, whose mission is to disintegrate our defects with a lance that she possesses.

No matter how diminutive these details may be, while manifesting, one must ask the Inner Divine Mother: **"My Mother, remove this defect and disintegrate it with your lance"**.

She will do so because that is Her mission, to help us so that we can liberate ourselves. In this way, the tree or Ego does not grow any more. It begins to lose its nourishment. It goes drying up.

What I am teaching here is for you to put it into practice, in real life: wherever you go, whether you are working or whatever you are doing, you must pay attention to your mind, to your heart and to your sex. Any defect manifest itself through each one of these three centers. When an element manifests itself, regardless of which of those three centers, you must immediately beseech your Divine Mother, so that she can proceed to disintegrate it.

Through this work on the death of the Ego that I am pointing out to you here, one acquires Scientific Chastity and one learns to love humanity. He who does not work on the disintegration of his psychological defects can never achieve chastity nor can he ever feel love for others, because he does not love himself.

The disintegration of the defects and the astral unfolding are the only formulas that exist for the rescue.

ASTRAL UNFOLDING

Dear Reader:

When we speak of the astral, consider if you have dreamed about people who have died years ago, about places and people that you do not know physically; that which people call common or ordinary dreams: 'Last night I dreamt such a thing.' But, nobody stops to think, 'Why was I dreaming of other places or locations, if my physical body was resting in bed?'

This is the Astral Plane or Fifth Dimension, to which the Astral Body belongs, where neither weight nor distance exist. This is a body exactly the same as the physical body. The Astral Body is energetic. It moves at great velocities like thought, capable of investigating whatever one wants in the Universe.

In the Fifth Dimension, we move, investigate and know what the Angels, the Virgin and all the Hierarchies are. The Hierarchies move, talk and teach

Wisdom that is not written in books. All this is beyond the human mind. When one wants to know for oneself that which people call Occultism, you can know it in the Fifth Dimension and it stops being occult.

What is important is not to leave the physical body with asleep-conscience, but to leave it with awaken-conscience and to move completely at will in the Fifth Dimension.

I am going to give you Mantras that I have practiced and that I know give positive results, for you my dear reader, to put Astral Unfolding into practice. A Mantra is a magical word that allows us to leave the physical body and to return to it with full Conscience.

First, lay down and relax your physical body. Second, pronounce one of these magical words or mantras three to five times, verbally and then you continue repeating it mentally. You will feel an electrical shock going through all of your body from feet to head, and that you seem to lose strength. Your body then enters a state of lassitude, and you do not want to move. Third, you must stand up with extreme care, without shaking yourself. After standing up, do a 'little jump' and at once you will find yourself floating.

Do not be afraid, surprised or overjoyed when you see yourself floating in the Astral Body. All human beings do this and nothing has happened to them. What happens is that they leave their bodies, unconscientiously. They do not do things at will.

All of us have our Divine Spirit, called Father. Once you see yourself floating in the air, say, 'My Father, take me to the Gnostic Church' or wherever you want to go to or know and He will take you there immediately, as quick as a flash. There you will receive the teaching directly from the Hierarchies.

That is how you go acquiring the true Wisdom, which is not written in books nor taught in the universities or anywhere else. I hope you practice it every night.

Mantra LA RA S: This Mantra is pronounced prolonging the sound of each syllable:

Lllllaaaaaaaaaaaaaaaaaaaaaaa
Rrrrrrrrrrrrrraaaaaaaaaaaaaaa (rolling the r)
Sssssssssssssssssss (like a whistle).

Another Mantra to leave Consciously in the Astral Body is:

FARAON

Faaaaaaaaaaaaaaaaaa Rrrrrrrrrrrrrraaaaaaaaaa Oooooooooooonnnnnnnnnn. (Rolling the r.)

I am going to impart another key for awakening Conscience in the superior dimensions:

Everything that we see here, that surrounds us, the houses, the people, the cars, have a double in the astral plane. When you want to know where you are, whether you are in the physical or in the astral, look around at the surroundings, the people, the houses, the place and ask yourself the following question: 'Why am I seeing such and such a thing? Making it feel strange to you, ask yourself again 'Is it that I am in the Astral Body or in the physical body?' Then do a 'little jump' with the intention of remaining floating.

You do not need to jump very high. You need to lift your body just a few centimeters off the ground to know if you are in the physical or not. If you do not float, it is because you are in the physical and if you do float it is because you are in the Astral Body. Then, upon seeing yourself floating, you must immediately ask your Inner Father to take you to the Gnostic Church or to the place that you wish to know.

Do it daily, as often as you can, at work or wherever you may be and you will see the results.

I sustain what I write in this book, because I know it. I am sure of what I say because I have investigated it thoroughly with my Astral Body, which allows me to know everything, meticulously.

FINAL NOTICE

I give these formulas to humanity, because whoever truly wants to save himself from the cataclysm that is coming must begin at once to disintegrate his psychological I, all the thousands of defects.

You must qualify, so that in the moment of rescue you will be taken to a safe place, where no harm will come to you and you can continue working on the Me-Myself, until reaching Liberation. The person who qualifies will be the one who succeeds in escaping from the disaster.

The Divine Justice calls this humanity 'the lost harvest.' That is to say there is nothing else to do. The destruction that is coming is because the Gods cannot do anything more for us. Therefore, no one can take the Hierarchy by surprise; everything is planned.

Dear reader, I am speaking very clearly so that you understand the necessity to seriously launch yourself to do the inner work, because whoever is working will be taken from the danger. This is not to be theorized or argued. Rather, the formulas that I am giving in this book are teachings you must experiment yourself, so you can go and get the Wisdom. There is nothing left to appeal to.

I am not a fear monger; I am a human being who is warning about that which will come. What I say is serious. Whoever has fear of God will begin to work against his defects, which keep us isolated from our inner Father.

Although I could go into more detail regarding the Esoteric part, I do not want to take up your time. Fight so that each one realizes this work that I teach, because it is the path to follow. I do not want anyone to be lost.